FAMINE CHAIR

SAINT JULIAN PRESS

POETRY

Also by Richard Jarrette

Strange Antlers

The Pond

The Beatitudes of Ekaterina

A Hundred Million Years of Nectar Dances

Beso the Donkey

Advance Praise—*Famine Chair*

What an awesome chair! Looks like it might want to join me on my daily walk. Would be perfect for when I need to take a break.

—Red Pine
Choosing To Be Simple: Collected Poems of Tao Yuanming
Zen Roots: The First Thousand Years

Richard Jarrette's voice is unique. I don't know anyone writing in a manner similar to his. There are echoes of Merwin, Rumi, the Chinese, but the texture and tone are all his own. The poems that pre-date *Beso the Donkey* are building to the miracle of what he accomplished there. But these have their own delights and mysteries, their illuminations and wonder. There is so much richness in his vision and a sense of the sacred along with an accomplished grace that is rare to find these days. It is wonderful to enter these poems (*A Hundred Million Years of Nectar Dances*).

—Joseph Stroud
Everything that Rises
Of This World: New and Selected Poems

Richard Jarrette combines erudition with profound simplicity and breathtaking beauty in *Strange Antlers*. He is a true disciple of the ancient masters, who can be heard and felt in these elegantly crafted poems full of poignancy and wisdom.

—Yun Wang
Dao De Jing, Laozi, Translated with Li-Young Lee
Dreaming of Fallen Blossoms: Tune Poems of Su Dong-Po

Advance Praise—*Famine Chair*

Famine Chair is not homage but an essential work of kinship. Richard Jarrette sits at a table with Red Pine, the classical Chinese and modern masters, and dines down to the marrow of a new poetry. Fifty years in the making, it is possible that poets in the far future will find these poems and be inspired to move their shared knowledge even further.

—Caleb Beissert
Beautiful - Translations of Lorca & Neruda

Red Pine and author with Camas Meditation Hall bell.

FAMINE CHAIR

Poems

by

Richard Jarrette

SAINT JULIAN PRESS
HOUSTON

Published by
SAINT JULIAN PRESS, Inc.
2053 Cortlandt, Suite 200
Houston, Texas 77008

www.saintjulianpress.com

ISBN-13: 978-1-955194-27-3
Library of Congress Control Number: 2024937764

Cover Art: Chinese birds and flowers (1430-1500)
vintage painting by Yin Hong from The Cleveland Museum of Art.

Photo Credits: Stancey Jarrette

To the cinnamon black bear sow
& for
Anne Carson
(who admonished)

CONTENTS

II Wheresoever (*Page 40–82*)

FAMINE CHAIR

Art – Stancey Jarrette

TOOL

It doesn't occur to me that my encounters with Red Pine/Bill Porter are the same as actual time with the classical Chinese poets and foundational teachers. It's just so. His plain-dealing, fulfilling translations bring me right here to the there-there. And I get to have some **BBQ** and whiskey with him and laugh a lot. He likes to wander through the old shipyard or lumber mill, somewheres like that, heading really toward a favorite food truck and brewery. Then my hand grasped his *Dancing with the Dead—The Essential Red Pine TRANSLATIONS* (Copper Canyon Press, 2023). On page 239, Liu Zongyuan memorializes an important confluence, "Meeting A Farmer at the Start of Spring"—

> I admire recluses but I'm not free
> nothing I try succeeds
> I related all this to a farmer
> explaining my situation in detail
> he kept rubbing the handle of his plow
> and turning to look at the looming clouds

which is something like walking about with Bill although he's more patient and good humored. "A hoe supplies a living," says Stonehouse (pg 67)—Red Pine's new book is yet another hand friendly tool for cultivating a life, it seems, before birth, now, and further?

My poor Irish ancestors often held one last chair after everything else had been laid in the fire, the famine chair. It was a rustic chair cobbled together from hedgerow sticks–storyful, survivor. That feels like the right posture for this cockeyed frame around Red Pine's marrow-deep work and its progeny, *Wheresoever,* which arrived when, after fifty years in all its weathers, Grass Mountain was my pulse and name. The conversation began with Red Pine's journey to China as an honored guest of the Vice Chairman and some commentary on it all at the time. It was good that friends joined our crew along the way such as Bob, Seamus, Homer, Alice, Lorca, and Rumi. As always, I imagine someone's about to throw a net over me for spilling all the way into this tango like I've done with donkeys, bees, and others who know their onions. And if Tao Yuanming appeared? Or Emperor Hadrian with that singular poem from the crucible of his life? Here's what happened. Thank you Bill, W. S. Merwin, Jane Hirshfield—and all come to say.

—*Cracked Patio*
Year of the Wood Dragon
Winter

FAMINE CHAIR

I

Dancing with Red Pine
Dancing with the Dead

where is that oriole singing
it hasn't stopped the whole time
—Tu Fu

1

Thinking Of Red Pine On His Way To China
As Honored Guest Of The Vice Chairman

Young aspen leaves
tell everything

full crows' nest high
in the ponderosa raucous

ripe dirty silver clouds
stray southeast

Any thought at all means trouble
says Stonehouse

2

Thinking Of Red Pine In China With The Vice Chairman
After Reading A Few Of The Stonehouse Translations

Moon
        clouds

did you arise from the Santa Inés
to climb Grass Mountain

river
        stars

the stick feels how deep
diamond willow

3

Red Pine Attempts To Avoid Hooks
Of The Politburo One Two Three Four

Eye blossom June flowers all over town
sweeten slight gray mist drizzle

government documents scuff up
a polished morning for awhile

it's a kingdom of shadows alright
Bob Dylan rasps an oldie

I'll stay right here and watch the river flow

4

High Hopes For The Ceremonial Toasts
Of The Vice Chairman And Red Pine

Moonlit Li Po cook Big Stick
maybe a few shimmers in my cup

I hope the Vice Chairman has a taste
for Red Pine's old whiskey

wouldn't it be good if he turned
to the tiger in the room and smiled

5

Red Pine's Liu Zongyuan
The Slough And The Beach

Sharp raccoon tracks circle tide pools
telling at the mouth of Pico Creek

night seas offered crab and snail golden
eagle in the monterey pine calculates

her claws like a Sumerian high-strung
ground squirrels in floodwood piles

enveloped by red-winged blackbirds
working their blarney in the horsetails

6

That's It So Far

Clouded peaks soothe the eyes
the work's already been done

thin or lush distant or near
leaves answer to the close airs

quiet bones have given over
grave duties and knotted will

to snowy willow catkins black
phoebes and a shy cricket

7

What's gone is already gone
             —Stonehouse

Mountain lilac *sierra blue*
startles a few spring days

the unmother a dying father
gleam in crow's other eye

pine cone windfalls fire
who knows what's coming

8

I Don't Think I Know My Onions Anymore

After fifty years at Tai Chi
the east foot corrects one inch north

demons smile

Monkey King lifts an eyelid
the glance at a duck

9

A thought breaks in the middle
             —Stonehouse

Move the battlefield to spare one ant
when fully practiced you won't
hear from me

10

Famine Chair

The garden's whatever comes
says a cabbage butterfly

down to one book by Red Pine
a real famine chair

prayer flags gone thready
all bleached out

11

Shoreless light lives on his lips
                              —Rumi

Dewdrop glint a basil leaf
perfumes its world

light spills into the dark corners
night and day

some teachers
you've let them in

one old poet told about
the mule he trusted

packing way out in the northern prairie
darkness sticks to everything

which was the light

12

Leave one unfraudulent hope
                    —Jane Hirshfield

Concrete driveway porch
weeds break through the cracks

bad ankle propped alongside
warty pumpkin on the table made

from a Liberty Ship hatch cover
the kid found on a beach

13

I sit on a rock by the pond and count fish
                              —Stonehouse

Lyrical willow catkins gone
high wispy clouds make blue blue

summer solstice day
Gascogne wine

fleeting raspberry and black currant kisses
orange and pink geranium boxes

who'll put off dead heading the roses
till Bastille Day

14

the clouds and moon go their own ways
                           —Puming

A few days into summer
clouds line up east to west

instead of north to south
gulls have their say

traveled waves rock the boy
barefoot till autumn

15

After Open Heart Surgery

Mourning doves settling
onto their limbs

sky your sorrow toward the waxing day moon
your soft landing lies beyond the clouds

cracks spreading in the concrete
steadfast hooves calm

Alice Oswald saying
Till rain gets into the stone

what was that one word

        dream poem

                    anyway

the ferryman leaned his cupped
ear close in

                waterful shadows

16

River Valley Airs

Vague colors murmur
as we climb the mountain
with river valley airs

few opinions will survive the fog

fat quail run dew laden
summer grass inclined
toward the Santa Inés

17

When I follow my nature I'm rash
                    —Wei Yingwu

Drawn outdoors
pieces of one black mind

crows

ragging on everything
those I love hurt I'm soul hurt

a lifetime following birds
arrived before myself

18

we saw each other and tried to talk
                    —Cold Mountain

Lift glass and nod earn
wary glances from crows

talk to them they'll fly off
to murder the west wind

man grapples crows perch
grooms regret but they

19

if I didn't follow the King of Emptiness
how did I end up here
                              —Stonehouse

A lot done ran to the trouble
asked now it's nothing doing

looky here midsummer again
backlit gnats the holy lights

not so sure how I survived
the rain of pianos to this chair

but here's some Stonehouse
and the flower stem set aside

it bookmarks the Red Pines
and a smooth beach rock

20

Cousins

Mind the forty-eight coyotes
within bay city limits

experts train people
to live with them

squid fishermen made
accords long ago

the alpha lopes by pre-
dawn without a glance

moves to neolithic song
we see the same river of stars

21

and the mountain mocks me for being so puny
                                        —Stonehouse

I stepped on a stone
a dried blood red stone

larricking along there in the tides
at the mouth of Pico Creek

maybe the eye of an iron mountain
come down to look at the sea

all the way
assayed by raccoons

otters and three curlews
stepped on it full weight

with a naked hoof like the cow
in Charles Simic's "Stone" *moo*

22

I wear myself out staying alive
                    —Stonehouse

Sometimes my jokes fall flat
maybe more than I know

I can be kind of edgy I guess
which cracks up my wife

He sharpens the butter knives

23

Widow Jane Bourbon

The bookmark keeps moving
to a favorite page of Red Pine's

Dancing With The Dead
reliving the BBQ and beers

and whiskey now pour some
pink Solimões River dolphins

24

it alone knows how cold the years have been
—Lin Zhen

Thomas Rain Crowe placed a white
cup by the sacred spring in Appalachia

suspicious bear panther ruby-throated
hummingbird day hikers gray fox kind

breathing marrow songs dogwood songs
our noble versions come weighing us

25

Across the countryside the grass extends for miles
he blows a few notes on the evening wind
—Lu Dongbin

Waves of sheen in flowering grasses
sweep over the ridge to vanish

into a close cerulean sky threads
of egret plume cirrus saying

twilight dawn rain will arrive
with southern ocean winds

Maria João Pires revealing Bach
fall to prayer in the fields and praise

26

Not nurturing new growth or getting rid of weeds
why doesn't he change his ways

—Qu Yuan

Sparring with killers the demon wars
rage-on-evil-death-wish in full flower

fifty years past a Tai Chi master said
till the movements have no meaning

screaky jays house finches bearing
witness eight generations from eaves

upset rooster serious dog cat gifts
of vole Norway rat and gopher lung

all these feline offerings for what
martial imitations of tiger and crane

or potluck with my shadow assassins
relentless as feral bindweed and wrath

27

Of W. S. Merwin
somewhere peach trees are blooming
—Stonehouse

A child
broken mother

violent father's sudden death
Animae opened to your tree talking

with little horse poem
shimmers of a lit chance

prayer

I hope you will come with me to where I stand
often sleeping and waking
by the patient water
that has no father nor mother

saludos heart-felt with Red Pine
agree all our volant

                praises

                        fall

dreams of animals the ancients gardens
uplifting their William

I belong to no one

28

no need to arrange a thing
                        —Stonehouse

Nothing in the blue blue
but blue this evening

graced by the whapping clothesline
sheets and cabernet sauvignon

inky black with concentrated
ripe stone fruits purring

something wants trouble come
lift a glass we already know

winter's going to rain through
that thin reputation again

29

after a snowfall the setting moon slips through the eaves
the shadow of a plum branch comes right to the window
                                            —Stonehouse

A regional blackout
sudden deep twilight used

fingers of cousin spirits rouse
mean after the wars

and demons took their share
cats at the window

nocturnal minds twitch
ghost of a rat

moon the crescent hay hook
takes the west

30

what will you do at death's door
                    —Cold Mountain

A surgeon opines *the bypass
good say ten years*

older now than my father ever was
so dead dead then

in his bed that morning
lit out to Cats Forest nest

a boy's run away

or was it Cold Mountain
lighting out toward the finding

31

how many frosty moonlit nights
have I sat and felt the cold before dawn
                              —Stonehouse

With the right jacket
you can sit in a snowstorm

at the crossroads
waiting for lost friends

and disappear like a lump
of Sierra Nevada granite

with a sweet Satsuma
orange in its pocket

32

when a moth puts out the altar lamp
                              —Stonehouse

A morning called the morning dream a deer's form in grass
there's a quarter day moon

the western cedar telephone pole flexing its arms with our busyness
seems to upraise that too

pale green wings brown eyespots one lit cabbage white
fans the sunny florets of a dandelion

33

A Breeze Takes Down The Heat

Eastward blown smoke
years at gardens

wearing out tools
not much today

track umbrella shade
eavesdrop on weather

34

and climb the peaks alone
                    —Shide

Grass Mountain named him Grass Mountain
to people it was Thrown Away

not in their saying but their doing
which made him a little crazy

that crazy wrote a lot of poems and this one
so maybe his real name is That Crazy

35

People ask the way to Cold Mountain
but roads don't reach Cold Mountain
                              —Cold Mountain

Fearful talk of screwworm
ghost panther North Fork River

cottonmouth under the bridge
last-born false courage goad

leap a shiver left of the rocks
through the serpent's wake

my father cared to pull over
on our way by the Mississippi

the gesture to swim across
he reckoned I could make it

red meat for a dog-like boy
eight years old water forever

36

the forest is secluded but partial to birds
                              —Cold Mountain

Branches try to take off in ten directions
the silent drama of a cabbage butterfly

labors north battling Pacific crosswinds
earning a cockeyed glance from one finch

gravity hasn't given up on me by noon
or sun certain I can be an O'Keeffe skull

37

the only difference is sooner or later
                              —Stonehouse

I don't know
a crow's thinking
until he's eating it

easier to read the minds of leaves

I seem to live
beneath disdain
best mind the eyes

38

perhaps we're from the same place
                              —Cui Hao

The kissing tree its deep reaching shade
we cooled Uncle John's team under the oak

plowed that down mountain dirt barefoot
for the high tasseling corn and field rye

heads dropped in a spring box like mules
we ate wild honeycomb with barlow knives

dealt out moonshine sack sugar and top leaf
from his skew-jawed barn by the path on

39

Actually there isn't a thing
much less any dust to wipe away
                    —Fenggan

Cells climb out of the ocean
rumors of deep things

star materials grasp beyond reach
everything yet happens

it all seems religious
in a glance of moonlight

the father in my pocket clenches
ten thousand years ago

loaded with plumeria flowers
the wind sweeps north

40

and the mountain's plum blossoms were still dreaming

—Red Pine

I don't know why the line makes me cry something
about Bill searching out Zhu Shuzhen's *resilience*

Seamus Heaney translating Sophocles for the funeral
of Czeslaw Milosz St. Catherine Church Kraków

light has gone out but the door stands open
Delft Blue appears as a late afternoon cloud's eye

among blues of 17th century Chinese porcelain
among pre-9th century Iranian *faience* whitenesses
terribly ambitious fraught say Zhu Shuzhen's eye
numberless eyes open her *Poems of a Broken Heart*

The weather was so warm it could have been spring
looking for plum blossoms I found a whole slope
breaking off a twig and sticking it in my hair
I laughed and asked "is anyone more shameless"

—Zhu Shuzhen

41

The room that was dark for a thousand years is suddenly full
of light

—Stonehouse

Gray squirrel snapping its tail
on a wire heading east

green grasshopper in the impatiens
poised by the front door

minunthadios
Homer said of Achilles and Hector
short-lived

speck of shattered glass
on the concrete patio

a glint between fast clouds
white Rose Window

42

looking at mountains without lowering the shade
—Stonehouse

It takes a blind caterpillar
to make a butterfly

with two eyes
seventeen thousand lenses each

43

A raging ox with menacing horns
runs away across hills and streams
—Puming

Rare August storm
all of a sudden mind lightning

Laestrygonians and Cyclopes savage Poseidon
bringing them along yes

ghastly strobing curtains one
Trojan War tramples on the next

collateral dead sewn into flags
waving in the just damage parade

darkened years rat-fleeing shame
the cast iron no exit cave boom

Four Horsemen of the Apocalypse
come spiriting their feral Enoch

my Schrapnellmine's scribe

Don't say I didn't warn you
says Stonehouse

44

the river's bends are as tortuous as my thoughts
—Liu Zongyuan

Clouds
silent singing severed Orpheus heads

good grief they have some weird stories
that boy jumped off a roof to the only safe

house in a time Cats Forest ground nest
first ever tropical cyclone west coast August

eight foot debris flows stranded firemen
now the earthquake you can't make this up

two rainbows after days of rain madly sky
it's blue O whitest burgeoning clouds

45

To Wei Yingwu

Trees
winds pass through

shiver and bend
wyrding fingers of mist

birds and butterflies live in there
winter the heavens

some make a springtime snow of catkins
seems like a kind of hilarity

or grief I don't know
people carve their names in the bark

that I can say is painful
for trees and men

we might remember that you said
I love unnoticed plants that grow beside a stream

46

the tiger tracks in the mud look fresh
                                 —Wei Yingwu
                          for S

Chronic ankle sprain unnerves
our birding of an evening

dropped by an assassin the madly crosshairs itch
lifelong cat and mouse stacked deck bastard

old for the canoe access cabin
we'll need a bigger house

with a room for Red Pine and a deft assistant
meds and indignities gathering clouds

still at three sharp we open a wine
that won't stop laughing

like the leaves when we forded Big Sur River
twice testing new boots

in riparian accord breathed touched
the alder and crossed again

47

In My Dream I Found An Abandoned
Sawtooth Ridge Cave And This Poem
Drawn On Rock With A Charred Stick

Sometimes you'll be the highwire
clown lurching wildly flapping

your arms and drop the umbrella
heed the Council of Crows one time

48

and a tiny star becomes a seed of trouble
                                    —Stonehouse

Ludicrous after all this motormouth
clouds not unserious

shifting the hidden into the more and more
waving the City of Monkeys flags

look at the mess of the sky
there's not enough old whiskey

can straighten it out tonight
crows yelling insults

before fucking off to their nighttime
roosts at Polliwog Pond

49

how long will my good years last
and why did I ever question my heart
                    —Tao Yuanming
          for A

My son glories the eggs conducts funerals
for his chickens and weeps

whither a world
tender more harsh

a bear was found sleeping in a tree
near white pelicans wintering in Los Osos

I could be found sleeping in a wheelbarrow
shaded by the white alders

creekside two acres of alluvial plain
lucky with gardens

50

A hoe supplies a living
          —Stonehouse

A neighbor's tool by the road
sharpened many a time

storyful in the hand alive
cultivates western airs

on the way to their door
remembering its gardens

with slender joy delivered
the hand keeps to cucumbers

51

flower smiles and bird songs reveal the hidden key
                                        —Stonehouse

She feeds bananas to the staghorn ferns
the whole world food for the whole world

wild rice baby bella mushrooms black garlic
this side of the horizon for now we laugh

Muhammad Ali said *I want something found*
right here on the ground while I'm still around

52

don't despair of this falling world, not yet
            didn't it give you the asking
                                        —Jane Hirshfield

So

nine hundred feet of drought killed
creek willows

restored with cuttings
submersed in trash barrels

filled with hose water
days of catkins flying three years

if spring

53

Such Poorly Cabbages

Lion Dog at the temple door
to protect the sacred

a little scary now
in the mirror falling

mismatched deaths
darkening news

uncaged monkey delusions
says Stonehouse

54

we blossom and fade like flowers
gather and part like clouds
                    —Stonehouse

Red Pine listen
come over to our place

lots of good food
and some new glasses

so elephant Tao Yuanming
will remember us

55

I'm truly mystified by this exchange
—Red Pine

Bee gives the toe a once over and leaves
fly vomits on the lip of my cup

knowing what can't be clarified
would save a lot of trouble

I imagine what you might say
and good old whiskey at the food truck

56

no wonder your poems chill a person's bones
—Wei Yingwu
for Caleb Beissert

Highlands brother hears a black
panther the Appalachian ghost

forest starlit shadow and frost
scream out there poet listening

other side of his glorious rye
feels the phantom slip his bones

as in Granada when the waiter
said *señor that's Lorca's chair*

57

I was even sized up by the dogs
                    —Cold Mountain

I fooled an old cowboy with my meadowlark call
he thought it worthy so conferred his brother's knife

was something for years after the ruse and proud
then a horse approached of an evening in the pasture

no carrot no fodder in her penetrating read of a man
another empty bag among stars in the mare's eye

58

The Truth that buddhas teach isn't learned by anyone
                              —Bodhidharma

Merciful golden fall light
finds my bones

bickering of age
cast in grief

against the white page
of the Bodhidharma wall

59

Jetavana's late autumn leaves are heavy
with a red much darker than blood
                              —Stonehouse

Ridiculous

Latin American jungle parrots
illegal imports India North Africa

burnt down pet shop survivors
squawk and shit all over the place

headsup under their tree
Irish French Scots Danish five percent

Neanderthal some Ashkenazi
stalks Red Pine

spraining the blood
harebrained and a nose beyond

cockeyed

60

Intoning Wei Yingwu With Gesture

Red Pine looks skyward
freshens the moment

hails the air with a goodly hand
sings something

about lighting out earlier
these shorter days

our horses whinny and keep turning their heads
they're glad to be going home

61

when all trace of our countless schemes disappears
                                                    —Cold Mountain

Fog making unmaking
this crescent moon

what sharpens dulls
our splendid tongues

autumn nights burn
Big Sur's dear swindle

62

do I have to wait for warfare to end
before comforting widows and orphans
                                    —Wei Yingwu

The unconverted moon rises over a satellite dish
corporate gladiators vie for billions on screens

a white government jet cuts the night for Panama
the CIA and Sun Tzu up there having cocktails

gravid airs lade stalks and limbs pulled down
seal barks dog answers from the sheer headland

63

A Glance At Red Pine's Wang Wei While Eating A Plum

for P

Savoring a tart fall plum
I remember leaving my wars

somewhere in the hills of hell
clashing among the poor demons

and remember sitting on a mid-
stream rock with a good son

who was working the fishhook
out of my finger with pliers

64

a song in which there is no Zen
                    —Cold Mountain

The sidewalk gave a Roosevelt dime
for daylong attention to the clouds

roiling complications east to west
by sundown empty lakes of sky

drifting north with a flock of gulls
low down crows shine a golden hour

65

Cold November Morning

Dirty silver cloud full of light
did you capture last night's

moon with the dream of a dog
son Zhuangzi said to father

and sleepy turtles who regard
their grapes and melon like old

scholars culling the forgeries
same as the morning mirror

66

from outside my door I can see the old mountains
                                        —Wei Yingwu

My friends gave me radiant gifts
right from their mouths

I accepted them fully
life was richer

I want to send you something
after the wars and injured years

but all I have left are these
ruined words

When last we said goodbye
the orioles were beginning to sing
—Tao Yuanming

II

Wheresoever

Grass Mountain

Grass Mountain named him Grass Mountain

Little Soul

after Hadrian

Little soul little stray
little drifter
now where will you stay
all pale and all alone
after the way
you used to make fun of things

—W.S. Merwin

windsound and moonlight wear away
one layer then another
                              —Stonehouse

Recluse
quiet
hears
the mountain
arrive

. . .

Leaf falls
left

shadow
right

blink
of the pendulum

a door

. . .

Tonight
the waxing
Blood Moon

unhindered
not knowing
its name

Abandoned
by two bees

for an empty
wine bottle

. . .

Gaze fixed
between ears
of a horse

neck turns
beyond the tail
a figure

mist

. . .

Ocean winds and riverine
valley heat marry

gyres present a condor
to Grass Mountain's *further*

Little soul

a person asks
what is a person

everything that is
everything that is not

never not answers
like walking on a mirror

and you down there
drifting off

wheresoever
whenever you feel like it

out of the frame
out of the question

.   .   .

Slope
of rocks

these crumbled
stairs

beautiful
seventy year

blunder

Raven Archilochos
crowns the power pole

above spider laying
her blood trap on

three wires to a house
close reading the air

     . . .

And bee
investigating
toes

what say
your dance
in the honey

     . . .

Two streams
flow into a lake

pierced a little
by light

near its mud
in the glance of a fish

the faint glint
of Venus

Rooster in the willows
crows overhead

mourning doves in the firethorn
having a parley

with the sun
after rains and hail

sweet toes on the serpent
fingers fleet at the loom Mary

.　.　.

Bulb set
little soul

dreaming
its glorious

blossom

.　.　.

The dry-paper
riffling buzzard feathers
louder

.　.　.

Also mortal
serpentine rock

lichens feeding
on your face

        . . .

The day gave a thin cry
and let down its wings

        . . .

Shipwreck storm
white pelicans

from the high plains
of central Canada

Big Sur jade
below the headland

treacherous
the secret caves

        . . .

Lone birdsong
silence

dust gathers
on the sea

late migrant
or too soon

strange weather
accidental

.   .   .

Winter birds
scratch in the ruins

mausoleum of sorrows
bitter candy

.   .   .

No eyelets
in the clouds

blackest night
little soul

feel the hand
at the loom

.   .   .

The sun appears white
in sharp January sky

its touch more precious
rufous-sided towhee

the black-hooded male
keeps to his promises

. . .

Winter's
mysterious colors

spring has yet
never said

. . .

Hidden blue road in blue sky
black in black

unfettered little soul

two hundred million butterflies
in the shape of an iron oak

. . .

Wilding
Coulter pines

broken
Hunger Moon

fingering
its hunger

. . .

Little soul

ghosting in the twilights
and faint birdsongs trailing off there

lips of horizons a brush
the pickpocket strange perfumes

glimpse at the edge-of-the-eye daughter's
cortège

toward

when the last resonant note in the cathedral dies
after the weeping and the knowing

the gathering trance

wasn't Homer right
a language known only to the gods

wheresoever

. . .

Now the moon winters a night of coyotes
and owls and the wet black calves

who will have to stand up and stagger
toward their mothers' moos in the pasture

. . .

The absence
of cabbage butterflies

you know this
butterfly

. . .

Others feed
the old big dog

who nonetheless
approaches

the empty hand
time after time

. . .

Vultures
overhang

after a sickly
late calf

. . .

Reading you little soul
something like fragments of Sappho

on garlic skin
after twenty seven hundred years

absent timeworn words crumbling in hand

] *holding the heart*
] *hear my prayer if ever at other times*
] *forsaking*

. . .

West wind
riffling dead leaves and grass

what mind
tender-curious

searching out the spring brides
at the graves

. . .

One hawk in a gyre
above the tallest pine

imagination perhaps
of blind roots deep

. . .

The crow says
evening has beautiful feet

spring poppies and yellow
bush lupine near

. . .

Two backlit mallards
heading north like crazy

not waiting for death
little soul

you never hole up
intimations nonstop

quit the job kiss those lips
laugh it off don't wait

do you hear death saying
fly together it's late

. . .

Today
everything
an enigma

today
a goshawk
the horse

. . .

The valley
washes mountain feet

with green hair
crows proclaim across

ridgelines
to their cuzzos

. . .

Amid big-cone pines
with the shakuhachi

Coast Range breathes
one thousand miles

. . .

Little soul
wheresoever runaway

a life with used eyes one tender
glances at spring's first blue bottle fly

pollinator of goldenrod and carrots
tasting a knuckle

flowering Grass Mountain offers a regard so sincere
the *4'33* of John Cage is five million years

through a transparent wing
you can see death's

furrow

. . .

Wildflowers rise
by the road

drivers slow down
for colors

and perfumes
fighting off hurry

to arrive
at their Ithakas

. . .

Rivers gone
three thousand years

take the mountain as mist
fill the lowlands

with silence
sheen on miner's lettuce

labors of Phoenician
oarsmen

. . .

It's complicated
weighing the soul of Jesus

Our Lady of Sorrows
dear *Yes* mercy

a person sinks like a person
drives home alone

from the celebration of life
in a silver car

pours wine into the black
cup etched *Nepenthe*

. . .

Toloache tells
in sacred caves

chosen by water
and the beings

painted *reveals*

. . .

Crested spring
bird green-black

core shadows to light
upslurred *hoooeet*

one one more
sumac berry

. . .

Where

directions
simple

somewhere
between

water
and duck

. . .

One shoe on the road
from layers of roads remembered

in a palm
has found one foot

you don't know why you'll limp a thousand years
through narrow versions of the world

until you find yourself
standing in the other shoe

. . .

Wild
spinning wind

transparent
dress

shamelessness
everywhere

an eagle
rides the river

on a boxelder
snag

. . .

Dear bird
the camouflage was working

to perfection
until the leaves all fluttered

not you

. . .

The ancient oak breathes night and day
inside its gnarled body sing the two

clouds and a hill a poet said the world
made of itself one May afternoon

. . .

Where
the violet-hued

hummingbird
withdraws its tongue

stills the wings
and dreams

. . .

It is apparent little soul
cows and lovers

and the skew-jawed
red roof shack

all fixing to drift off as in the Chagalls
Thelonious Sphere Monk

Ruby, My Dear
followed on my *Crepuscule*

With Nellie (Take 6)
and then with divine logic

(Takes 4 and 5)
more poppies have opened

in the riverine valley
it's out of hand

. . .

Walking barefoot on pepper fruit husks
summons the white dragon

streaming a hundred miles of banners
heading north with a Phoenix

reading the world with its left eye
hunting for the daughter's fever demon

. . .

Green lion
night and day

has been here
unseen

until buteos
circling

. . .

Little soul a legged red
dot it's a spider

running the margins
as if to escape spider Furies

sparrows scratch for seeds
gone flowers back

raise nectar toward the hive
queen out of the gully

quail chasing his plume
through dry grass

. . .

Among us
wilier than the shadow of a rat

children
you understand

welcome the dear hidden
into your Planh

bobcats and wild pigs
foxes and bears

little soul

like the liner notes to Coltrane's
Olatunji Concert:

The Last Live Recording
down at the bottom

of personnel
Juma Santo—percussion

(possibly)

.   .   .

One share
of light

to be returned
wheresoever

.   .   .

The realization
it all makes sense

executioner poised
one step behind

knees petition dust
branch nods

. . .

Rain nears
mountain lilacs stir

highland grasses
ready to lift

stalks and seeds
a little more

and it's possible
something never seen

could appear
and show its flower

. . .

Twilight
murmurs

new moon
quiet owl wings

limning
little soul

the reach

   . . .

Poplars leaning together
mind leans

pale mulberry catkins
like eyebrows

from *Eyebrow Mountain*
in the west

   . . .

Mites work deeper into the skins
of the barnyard ducks

waddling near the old blind dog
having a scratch at his hide

where it is now where it's been
an all-knowing moan in his throat

   . . .

Crazy windchimes
yield to deeper listening you say

Figueroa Mountain shaking Coulter pine cones
big as pineapples

rattling the claws of the cinnamon
black bear sow

.   .   .

Two great horned owls
confer pine to pine

five notes open south
four answer north

experienced dog
comments and offers

the moment to a man
let loose your longing

.   .   .

Well hidden the moon
between your eyebrows

.   .   .

Little soul
all asked

all not asked
all present

all absent
all the promise

. . .

Officers of Inquisition
scourged and burned

women of entire regions
to repudiate soul

but they've still failed
at killing Angela Davis

. . .

Nothing waits
for permission

in the wind
grass to cloud

seeing medicine

. . .

Sun
moon

Cygnus
cold

lake
willing

. . .

Threat
in the server's smile

Sappho's
unmanageable creature

egyptian violet nails
shame torn from pierced tongue

and fine birds brought you
quick sparrows over the black earth

unfettered
the quickening

. . .

Driven to the morally serious
by fires and drought scrub jays

the upland planters bury more
acorns than they remember

. . .

Hadrian said
you make fun of things

little soul

what about rage
this lust for killing

unless the questions
your answer

this time
the breath it takes

one rest
in the measure

two

.   .   .

A heart of stone
filled with fire

required says
the stone world

against enemies
but moonlight

.   .   .

Little soul
daimon of the wrong turn

chance encounter
whistling

the resistance

marriage abandoned
friends lost

raccoons take granddaughter's
chickens

a massacre

they were hungry too
she says

. . .

Sun
sweet-cruel

lord of days
this day

come closer
with your chariot

and horses
or beetle

. . .

Jewel in the grass
froggy carries a moonlit
glimmer of July

                              . . .

Thok of the maple
on oak gate latch

obsessions locked out
Euripides captures them

others hold the altar
dusted dusted

an Aiskhylos of crows
telling telling

                              . . .

Seen through a spider's web between wires
silver airliners flying people to New York

one after another daylong it happened
everything in the *one square inch* happened

                              . . .

Black cat makes
no move on the jays

they've settled on a ten foot
boundary at all times

isn't that about right little soul
all these calculations

when whosoever
shows up at the saloon

.   .   .

An evening sky
of a pearl's lustre

largest pearl ever
trees west a violet

shade impossible
for human eyes

.   .   .

Night
and day

light
through

thin
keyhole

.   .   .

Your moonful presence
feels like love

little soul

as a face turns
and is turned

relentless for the hidden side

. . .

Do you sleep in the body
suspended like a sperm whale

in the deeps send your dark
songs ten thousand miles

seeing the blue veins exposed
by a pregnant dog who bit

and dragged the careless boy
you were terrible and near

. . .

Crow's
intense cockeye

of the not hidden
to crows

. . .

Gnat on the large world
backlit fairy speck

against deep forest
loom of origins psalter

spark of almost knowing
glimpse dear viejo

.   .   .

Pond reeds
egret

one
gullet

swaying
just so

.   .   .

It's amazing little soul
how you flow like water around things

become the meaning each shape is

reveal like Scriabin
around things

.   .   .

Guttering candle
small room

Rachmaninoff
the restored pages

his friends said were
just too much

. . .

Eerie winds
take live oaks

into some not-
human ecstasy

the little lusts
of the birds

. . .

Asked after
the listening hand lifted

what a three thousand
year tree said

the suppliant faltered
unable to stand

. . .

Are you muddied by the violence
and wars in a person

eyes sealed by shame
blind face in the mirror

condemning itself
with precision little soul

though black phoebes nest and flutter
so close again this year

. . .

The ethics the mind
of Confucius and Lao Tzu

Dragons of Heaven
yet noble Ch'ü Yüan

failing to save the nation
drowned in despair

. . .

You wouldn't say
just collateral damage

your thunder keening
impossible

. . .

Silver and gray-black clouds part
descending breezes play the valley

with father sky's autumn light
songs of lamentation lift golden

. . .

Sunny coffeeberry lucence
leaves' pale undersides telling

wrentit fights the wind upslope
heart following eye to bush

. . .

The spare
crescent moon

knife thrower
slips through Coulter pines

tracked by slim-waisted
highland coyotes

over Mule Ridge
to the farms

. . .

Languid pulsing cloud
no consensus

on what adds up to be a gnat
little soul

like you

though classified
biting or non-biting

but may it happen to me [

all [

Sappho thrums

. . .

Mountain to mountain
vasty blue

river valley uplifted
by two red tails

into the absence
beyond the north wind

. . .

Rough seas
where everything
seems to be coming from

two ducks
a little ways beyond
blowholes and churns

gnarled rocks
with woman adoring
the one pedicel

. . .

Cabbage white toiling north
disappears into tree

crow shoots out hard
flaps heading south

maybe about the earthquake
last week and the next

. . .

Some days
a cat

on the dragon's
knees

. . .

One bee
cactus wren

strange
weather

unmanageable
hymn

and thee

. . .

Cream moonlight
coyotes'

prey the abandoned
little soul

. . .

Autumn sun-heat
intensifies rose hips

and the last red
geranium blossom

truing salty west
wind off the Pacific

. . .

Buddha's open palm
gesture on the windowsill
nineteen rain crows say

. . .

Early winter
clarifies living

bare sycamore
among evergreen

ordained god-
hungry raptors

the grasp

. . .

This talk about souls
around the dead

everlasting glory
communion eternal

rise up shake the devil out
immortal are we

little soul
from wrath saved

. . .

It was the Pleiades
at the river mouth

. . .

One horse in a column of light
sets the holy pace

stillness

draws a mark on the forest floor
with its right front hoof

. . .

Asking of you
little soul

a walk on the wind
what is this

gaze fixed on
Grass Mountain

what is this
Grass Mountain

gaze fixed on

————————

ACKNOWLEDGMENTS

I thank my wife, Stancey, who endured endless revisions on the patio, without a shred of impatience, and for her exquisite thread art gracing this book. Hats off to Red Pine for friendship and fine, plain-spoken works that have shaped not only my poetry but my self. Thank you Copper Canyon Press and Empty Bowl for publishing Red Pine's essential work and so beautifully. Jane Hirshfield's steady friendship, and penetrating comments on my work and beyond, have been vital to my peace of mind—her poetry woven seamlessly with the classical Chinese masters and borrowed with joy. I am honored to know Yun Wang, Poet/Translator/Cosmologist, with gratitude for her poetry, translations of Su Dong-Po, Laozi, and *Beso the Donkey*, and for her surveys of galaxies and investigations into dark energy. My appreciation for Ron Starbuck, Saint Julian Press, will persist—such fine, unrestrained, understanding and dedicated work. I thank all of my teachers, particularly my sons Amos and Peter.

NOTES

I
Dancing with Red Pine/*Dancing with the Dead*

Epigraph one
The Zen Works of Stonehouse (1999) Red Pine, Note 98.1, pg 212.
Epigraph two
Finding Them Gone (2016) Bill Porter/Red Pine, Tu Fu, "Climbing to Oxhead MountainTemple" pg 138.

1. *Dancing With The Dead—The Essential Red Pine Translations* (Copper Canyon Press, 2023) Red Pine, 6 Stonehouse, <u>*Any thought at all*</u> pg. 59, hereafter all *DWTD* unless indicated.
   —*What a fine sendoff. What could go wrong?*
   —*More whiskey.*
   —*Likely not enough.*

2. —*Thinking of Richard thinking of Red Pine thinking of Stonehouse not thinking. Tea is ready, and it's now watching the vice premiers in the Politburo Pond, <u>one, two, three, four</u>. I wonder what they're thinking . . . or if they think at all, swim around avoiding <u>hooks</u>.*

3. "Watching The River Flow" *Bob Dylan's Greatest Hits II*—*Think I'll sit on the shore and fish today. 6/06/23, morning in China*

4. <u>*Big Stick*</u> (Fenggan), Cold Mountain's friend, appeared at Guoqing Temple accompanied by a <u>*tiger*</u> and became the head <u>*cook*</u>. Sometimes the great matter is old whiskey, sometimes old whiskey is the great matter.

5. After Liu Zongyuan, "5 Ode for a Caged Eagle" pg 237.

6. After Stonehouse 66, page 67.

7. 89 Stonehouse, pg 69 . . . *right now I'm writing a right-now line.*

9. 60 Stonehouse, pg 66.

10. —*Must be eyesight, the poems just keep getting better, 7/21/23.*

11. Rumi *Gold* (2022) Haleh Liza Gafori Translator, pg 38; <u>*Darkness Sticks to Everything*</u> (Copper Canyon, 2013) Tom Hennen, pg 13—and personal correspondence.

12 *The Asking* (2023) Jane Hirshfield, "Manifest" pgs 6-7.

13. 118 Stonehouse, pg 74.

14. Puming, "VIII Forgetting the Other" pg 20.

15. *sky your* a year's production post heart attack; *Dart* (2002) Alice Oswald, *Till* Line 9 pg 10.

17. Wei Yingwu, "76 Planting Melons" pg 185.

18. 134 Cold Mountain, pg 38.

19. 70 Stonehouse, pg 67, and *70 Note: The Buddha is the King of Emptiness.*

20. *we see the same river* Wei Yingwu, "95 New Fall Night: To My Cousins" Line 2 pg 186.

21. 91 Stonehouse, pg 70; *Falling Awake* (2016) Alice Oswald, "Dunt: A Poem For A Dried-Up River" pg 35 *the two otters larricking along*; *Quite Early One Morning* (1945) Dylan Thomas, "Holiday Memory" *larrikin* invented from Welsh or Irish/Australian—a young man who goes about drinking and getting into scrapes *Lolling or larriking that unsoiled boiling beauty of a common day, great gods with their braces over their vests sang, spat pips puffed smoke at wasps, gulped and ogled, forgot the rent*; *Dismantling the Silence* (1971) Charles Simic, "Stone" pg 59 *Even though a cow steps on it full weight* . . . .

22. 85 Stonehouse, pg 68.

24. Lin Zhen, "166 Cold Spring Pavilion" pg 165; Thomas Rain Crowe (b.1949), poet, translator, editor, publisher, recording artist, environmentalist, preserver and gift giver of sacred Southern Appalachian lands which he cherishes and protects.

25. Lu Dongbin, "175 Herd Boy" Poems of the Masters, pg 166; Maria João Pires, *Partita No. 1*, Bach, Deautche Gramophone (2002) *fall to prayer in the fields and praise*—imagining Bach's feeling.

26. Qu Yuan, "from *A Shaman's Lament*: Beset by Sorrow" Lines 21-22 pg 268; *rage* Note #53.

27. 57 Stonehouse, pg 66; *Animae* (Kayak, 1969) W.S. Merwin, George Hitchcock Publisher, "Little Horse" *I belong to no one . . . I hope you will come with me to where I stand . . .*; Merwin's garden labors will flower a long time to come.

28. 66 Stonehouse, pg 67.

29. 96 Stonehouse, pg 70; (Grenache Rose 2022, San Simeon, Paso Robles).

30. 234 Cold Mountain & Friends, pg 44.

31. 107 Stonehouse, pg 72; *Satsuma*—hybrid mandarin/pomelo, November-February harvest.

32. 117 Stonehouse, pg 73; *dream a deer's form in grass*—archaic French *meuse*.

34. 49 Shide, Cold Mountain & Friends, pg 52.

35. 16 Cold Mountain & Friends, pg 29. See note #56—Appalachian Black Panther.

36. 31 Cold Mountain & Friends, pg 32.

37. 131 Stonehouse, pg 74.

38. Cui Hao, "15 Ballad of Changgan" pg 149; *top leaf* potent uppermost tobacco leaves.

39. 4 Fenggan, Cold Mountain & Friends, pg 49.

40. Of Zhu Shuzhen, pg 227 Lines 3-4 and from pgs 221-229
     Her parents were so embarrassed by her talent, they burned all the poems they could find after she died. Lucky for us, someone gathered copies she shared with friends, over three hundred of them, and titled the resulting collection Poems of a Broken Heart pg 228; *The Translations of Seamus Heaney* (2023), "Testimony: What Passed at Colonus" pg 92; *Faience or faïence* is the general English language term for fine tin-glazed pottery— a white pottery glaze suitable for painted decoration, by the addition of an oxide of tin to the slip of a lead glaze, a major advance in craft.

41. *The Zen Works of Stonehouse* (1999) Red Pine, "Zen Talks" Lines 11-12 pg 189; *The Iliad* (2023), Emily Wilson Translation, "Introduction" pg xi, *minunthadios*.

42. 16 Stonehouse, pg 60.

43. Puming, "Untamed" pg 13; *Laestrygonians . . .* from Cavafy's "Ithaka" a version; *Four Horsemen*—amygdala, hippocampus, cerebellum and pre-frontal cortex; *Enoch*—*scribe of judgement*, son of Jared, great-grandfather of Noah; Genesis 5:18-25; *The Book of Enoch*, *Schrapnellmine*—landmine that leaps up, whistles, erupts; *The Zen Works of Stonehouse* (1999) Red Pine, "Zen Talks" *Don't say* Lines 18-23 pg 189—and see poems #1 & #53.

44. 106 Liu Zongyuan, "Climbing Liuchou Tower—Sent to the Magistrates of Zhang, Ding, Feng, and Lian Counties" pg 258.

45. 110 Wei Yingwu, "Chuzhou's West Stream" pg 187.

46. *The Poetry of Wei Ying-wu: In Such Hard Times* (2009) Red Pine, "Mounting Up to Go Back After Traveling in the Mountains in Heavy Rain" pg 301.

48. *The Zen Works of Stonehouse* (1999) Red Pine, "Zen Talks 22" pg 141 and Note 22.2 pg 140 *According to the account of Shakyamuni's life in the "Lahtavistara Sutra," his Enlightenmnent occurred when he beheld Venus on the western horizon; … but who cares / the Yangste rolls on / the sun and moon don't slow their pace / and all you do is sit on your beds / while a black dragon lurks in the clouds* pg 142 Note 25.5 and "Zen Talks 25" Lines 10-12 pg 143.49. 4 Tao Yuanming, "Held Up at Guilin by Winds While Returning from the Capital in the Fifth Month of 400 II" Lines 11-12 pg 302; *Los Osos— the bears,* grizzlies have been exterminated but a population of black bears live nearby in Los Padres National Forest; white pelicans and monarch butterflies winter in the area beginning September-October.

50. 66 Stonehouse, pg 67; *Where joy most revels, grief doth most lament: Grief joys, joy grieves, on <u>slender</u> accident* Shakespeare, *Hamlet* III ii.

51. 36 Stonehouse, pg 63; Muhammad Ali, personal communication, 1970.

52. *The Asking* (2023) Jane Hirshfield, "Counting, New Year's Morning, What Powers Yet Remain To Me" pg 4; *So* homage Seamus Heaney's *Beowulf* (2001), his solution to *Hwæt!*

53. *The Zen Works of Stonehouse* (1999) Red Pine, 68 Stonehouse, <u>uncaged</u> pg 35; Jane Hirshfield once helped with my *<u>rage</u>*: "It's understandable, just remember what it's supposed to protect, like those fierce beings guarding temples in Asia" (#26, #43).

54. 31 Stonehouse, pg. 62; *so elephant* a mishearing of *so inelegant,* which stands.

55. *The Zen Works of Stonehouse* (1999) Red Pine, Note 98.1, pg 212, worth repeating.

56. 28 Wei Yingwu, "On My Day Off Visiting Censor Wang and Finding Him Gone" pg 176   *no wonder your poems chill a person's bones / your door faces an icy stream and snow-covered hills;* Appalachian Black Panther, *painter,* still appears here and there to some.

57. 220 Cold Mountain & Friends, pg 43.

58. *The Zen Works of Stonehouse* (1999) Red Pine, "Zen Talks" Bodhidharma quote, Line 14 pg 219. How many years did Bodhidharma glare at his cave wall, anyway?

59. *The Zen Works of Stonehouse* (1999) Red Pine, "To Attendant Ch'ang Writing the Diamond Sutra in Blood" Gathas 52, pg 113 *The Buddha preached the Diamond Sutra in Jetavana* Note pg 112.

60. *The Poetry of Wei Ying-wu: In Such Hard Times* (2009) Red Pine, pg 301.

61. 275 Cold Mountain & Friends, pg 46.

62. Wei Yingwu, "On First Reaching This Prefecture" Lines 19-20 pg 194; Israel-Hamas War begins October 7, 2023. Wei Yingwu faced war refugees and chaos Jiangzhou 785 (c.e.).

63. Wang Wei, "77 Passing Xiangji Temple" pg 154. I misread the line: *somewhere in the hills a bell* as <u>*somewhere in the hills of hell*</u>—where I spent many formative years.

64. 282 Cold Mountain & Friends, pg 47.

66. 38 Wei Yingwu, "Describing My Feelings to Commandant Lu" pg 177.

Postscript *Choosing To Be Simple—Collected Poems of Tao Yuanming* (Copper Canyon Press, 2023) Red Pine, "56 In Reply to Advisor Pang V" pg 239.

NOTES

II
Wheresoever

Epigraph 1—W.S. Merwin, "Little Soul" from The Shadow of Sirius. Copyright © 2008 by W.S. Merwin pg 51, and see pg 114 "Animula: A Late Visitation" on his lifelong work with that one poem attributed to Emperor Hadrian (A.D. 76-138). Reprinted with the permission of The Permissions Company, LLC on behalf of Copper Canyon Press www.coppercanyonpress.org. All rights reserved. And see also *Ledger*, Jane Hirshfield (2020), "AMOR FATI" pgs 91-98 for her *little souls*—first after Hadrian.

Epigraph 2—*The Zen Works of Stonehouse*, Red Pine (1999) pg 51, and at <u>one square inch</u> see the Stonehouse pgs 6-7—one might hear echoes of the Master here and there throughout.

<u>*toward*</u>—*Economy of the Unlost*, Anne Carson (1999) pg 62 (71) *Simonodes' claim is more radical, for it comprehends the profoundest of poetic experiences: that of "not" seeing what "is" there.*

Sappho quotes and ghosts—*If Not, Winter: Fragments of Sappho*, Anne Carson (2002) Nos. 42, 47, 63, 86, 94, 130, and 177.

<u>*Toloache*</u> (*datura inoxia*, relative *wrightii*) moon flower, thorn apple, sacred datura, jimsonweed, chamico, Nahuatl—"bow the head."

Eros the Bittersweet (1986) Anne Carson—*(Eros) exists because certain boundaries do. In the interval between <u>reach and grasp,</u> between glance and counterglance . . . the absent presence of desire comes alive* pg 30.

Sorry sweetmeat for <u>the little lusts of the birds</u>—Sophokles Antigone, Anne Carson Translation (2015) pg 13.

Red Pine, Grass Mountain, and deer.

ABOUT THE AUTHOR

RICHARD JARRETTE's formative years were spent in the Southern Appalachian Highlands of Western North Carolina, where he is considered a regional writer, and then in the Central Coast of California and its mountains. His poetry is informed by comprehensive landscape life cycles, alongside the influences of classical Chinese poets and foundational teachers. *Beso the Donkey* (2010) received the Gold Medal for Poetry from the Midwest Independent Publishers Association and was translated into Chinese by Yun Wang. Jarrette is retired from a forty-five-year psychotherapy career and is a practitioner of Tai Chi. His poems arrive in river valley weathers of the San Rafael Range, Chumash Lands, and on Pacific winds of Big Sur.

Printed in the USA
CPSIA information can be obtained
at www.ICGtesting.com
LVHW081914110724
785247LV00044B/1138